The Stuff of Legend™

Book 3: A Jester's Tale

Story by
Mike Raicht & Brian Smith

Illustrated by
Charles Paul Wilson III

Design & Color by
Jon Conkling & Michael DeVito

WWW.TH3RDWORLD.COM

The Stuff of Legend is a work of fiction. Names, characters, places and incidents are the products of the authors' imaginations or are used fictitiously. Any resemblance to actual events, locales or persons, living or dead, is entirely coincidental.

2012 Th3rd World Studios Trade Paperback Edition.

Published in the United States of America by Th3rd World Studios, Inc.

The chapters in this book first appeared in the comic book The Stuff of Legend - Volume 3: A Jester's Tale, © and TM 2011 by Mike Raicht, Brian Smith, Charles Paul Wilson III and Th3rd World Studios and published by Th3rd World Studios.

ISBN 978-0-9832161-2-4

Printed in Korea.

9 8 7 6 5 4 3 2 1

Publishers
Michael DeVito
Jon Conkling

WWW.TH3RDWORLD.COM

Special thanks to
Brock Heasley

The Stuff of Legend™

Chapter 1:
An Unlikely Pair

The North Clove Sea
WE'VE GOT HIM CORNERED, BOYOS!
NO WAISTER ATTACKS THE BOOGEYMAN'S FLEET AND LIVES T'TELL THE TALE!
ALL HANDS, SEND HIM TO THE DEPTHS!
POOM!
CONSTABLE'S HOOK

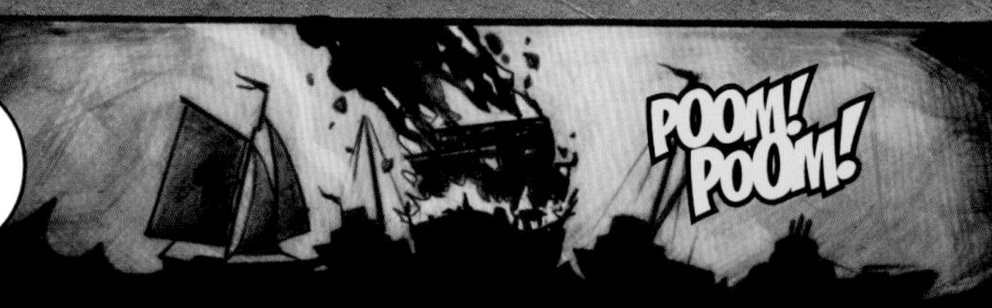
COME 'ROUND THERE -- CLOSE THAT GAP!
THE *KNOCKABOUT* AND HER CAPTAIN WON'T ESCAPE US THIS NIGHT!
POOM! POOM!

NOW, YA SPROGS! STORM THE DECKS!

SNAP!

BOOM!

BACK! GET THAT DEMON OFF MY SHIP!
BLEED HIM!

CANNONS READY! SCUTTLE THE HUDSON--
NO CAPPY, NOT OUR OWN...

FIRE, YA LOT OF MARYS! FIRE OR I'LL HANG YA FROM THE TOPMAST MESELF!
ORDERS'RE TO DEFEND OUR CARGO, NO MATTER THE COST. THEM'S THE BOOGEYMAN'S WORDS!
AYE, CAPPY!

POOM!
'S HOOK

BOOM!
HUDSON

LOOK-- THERE! ***HE LIVES!***
BRACE YOURSELVES--

HUK!
GAAH!

AAAAH!
ABANDON SHIP!
COWARDS! BEST HOPE THE DEEP CLAIMS YA, LEST I FIND YA FIRST!
CONSTABLE'S HOOK

CONSTABLE'S HOOK
FSSSSSSSH...

BA-BOOOOM!

GAH! BLASTED SEA DEVIL... YA WON'T GET AWAY WITH THIS!

YOU WOULD STEAL HIS PROPERTY? THE BOOGEYMAN'LL HAVE YER HEAD! WHAT DO YE WANT!?!

THE BOY.
BLAM!

1

Elsewhere, deep within The Jungle
PRINCESS!
THERE YOU ARE. MAXWELL HAS BETRAYED US ALL. THE ANIMALS HAVE CROWNED HIM KING! PERCY AND THE OTHERS INTEND TO LEAVE THE DARK.
OUR CRUSADE IS AT AN END. THE BOY WILL DECIDE HIS OWN FATE...
ARTIC! WHAT TRANSPIRES HERE? EVEN YOUR BAIT IS CURIOUSLY QUIET.
WHY THE SILENCE, MAYOR? NO GLOATING IN THE FACE OF OUR FAILURE?
BITING YOUR TONGUE WON'T SAVE YOU NOW. QUITE THE CONTRARY! ONCE THE BEASTS GET WIND OF YOUR STENCH I SEE QUITE A BIT MORE BITING IN YOUR FUTURE.
I SHALL TEND TO YOUR WOUNDS, PRINCESS. AND WHEN YOU ARE WELL, WE WILL PLAN OUR NEXT MOVE TOGETHER.

PRINCESS...?
NO!

A TRICK?!?
FWIP!

OH JESTER...
YOU ARE
A FOOL.
WHSSSSHHH

SMMMAAAACK!
UNNGH!

"QUIET, YOU DOLT!"
The Ruined Zoo
YOU NEVER LISTEN TO ANYONE, PERCY.
THIS IS HARDLY THE TIME TO DEBATE MY LEADERSHIP SKILLS.

HE HAS A POINT, QUACKERS. PLEASE... THIS DISCUSSION CAN WAIT.
AND WHY DO YOU ALWAYS TAKE HIS SIDE, HARMONY? I SAY WE CAN SNEAK RIGHT BY THESE MUGS.
NOT ALL OF US CAN FLY, YOU GLORIFIED FEATHERDUSTER. LEAVE THE PLANNING TO ME.

RIGHT. CAUSE YOU'VE BEEN DOING SUCH A BANG-UP JOB SO FAR.
OF ALL THE UNGRATEFUL... HAVE YOU FORGOTTEN HOPSCOTCH? WHERE I SAVED EVERYONE? OR DO YOU STILL WISH YOUR BEST FRIEND WERE IN CHARGE?

MAX IS AS GOOD AS DEAD TO ME NOW, YOU JERK!
FOLLOWING HIM NEARLY GOT ME COOKED. I'M DONE FOLLOWING ANYBODY.
LOWER YOUR VOICE!

QUACKERS, DON'T...
QUACKERS!

WHUSSAT... WHO'S THERE?
IT'S THEM. THE RENEGADE TOYS!

KILL THEM ALL!
BLAM!

NO-- WAIT! LET ME EXPLAIN! THE BOOGEYMAN--
WANTS YOUR HEAD, PIGLET. I AIM TO PROCURE IT.

GAAAAH!

TAKE THEM DOWN.
MAKE IT HURT.
MY EYES!

DIBS ON THE COWBOY.
R-ROSE?

NO MORE SHOOTING.
UUUNNGH!
SLAAM!

GOOD WORK, JACQUES.
WHAT IS THE MEANING OF THIS? WHY ARE YOU FOLLOWING US, ROSE? HAS MAXWELL SENT YOU TO FINISH US OFF?
KING MAXWELL.
GRRR... EAT HIS SNOUT, BROTHER. HIS SQUEALING OFFENDS.

BRAM! BRIAR! CONTROL YOURSELVES.
HOLD, SISTER. THIS ONE WILL HAVE TO WAIT.
YES, BROTHER.

WHAT ARE YOU DOING HERE, ROSIE?
ROSE.
DON'T GET ME WRONG, IT'S GREAT TO SEE YOU AND ALL... BUT...
YOU'RE NOT HERE TO KILL US, ARE YOU?

WE ARE HERE TO HELP YOU ON YOUR FOOL'S ERRAND. OUR NEWLY CROWNED KING ASKED THAT I SEE YOU ESCORTED SAFELY OUT OF THE DARK, AS IF THAT IS A POSSIBILITY...
DO NOT MAKE ME REGRET ACCEPTING THIS TASK ANYMORE THAN I ALREADY DO.

COME. THERE WILL BE MORE SOLDIERS. GATHER YOURSELVES QUICKLY, AND TRY TO REMAIN SILENT.
WAIT FOR **ME**, BEAUTIFUL!
SO MUCH FOR SILENT.

OOOHHHH...
JESTER! THIS IS NO TIME FOR A NAP!

WAKE UP, YOU ***BUFFOON***! ARTIC HAS TAKEN THE PRINCESS!

...MY HEAD... LOWER YOUR VOICE.

MY THANKS FOR YOUR WARNING, VILLAIN.
ANY QUALMS I HAD ABOUT LEAVING YOU TO ROT HAVE VANISHED.
WHAT!?!

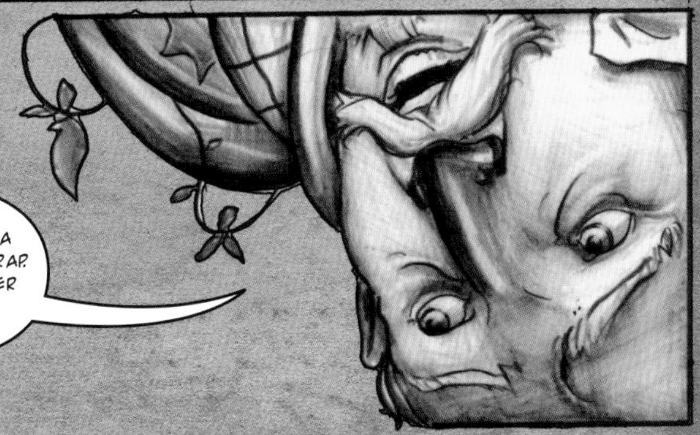
THAT SCOUNDREL ARTIC, HE BEAT ME 'TIL I LOST CONSCIOUSNESS-- ME, A DEFENSELESS MAN! I WOULD HAVE ALERTED YOU IF I COULD!
TRUTH BE TOLD, IT WAS A FAIRLY OBVIOUS TRAP. I WON'T SHOULDER ALL OF THE BLAME.

MAGNANIMOUS TO THE LAST! DO SAY HELLO TO THE JACKALS FOR ME. TA-TA!
WAIT! LET'S BURY THE HATCHET, JESTER. I CAN TAKE YOU TO THE INDIAN LANDS! THAT'S WHERE YOU'LL FIND ARTIC AND YOUR PRINCESS.

I WILL FIND MY OWN PATH.
MORE LIKELY YOU WILL END UP IN THE BOOGEYMAN'S CLUTCHES.
THE JOURNEY IS FRAUGHT WITH PERIL... IF IT'S ANY CONCILIATION, I'LL MOST LIKELY DIE ALONG THE WAY.
YOU'LL NEVER FIND HER WITHOUT ME!
BAH! ENOUGH!

AS MUCH AS IT PAINS ME TO ADMIT, YOU MAY STILL PROVE USEFUL.
HEAR ME NOW. IF YOU ATTEMPT TO DECEIVE ME, EVEN ONCE, I WILL GLADLY ACCEPT YOUR OFFER TO BURY THE HATCHET... DEEP WITHIN YOUR SKULL.

YOU WON'T REGRET THIS!
THWAP!
THAT REMAINS TO BE SEEN.

THANK YOOOOOWCH!
WHUMP!

HO-HO! THIS WAY, MY BOY-- NARY A SECOND TO SPARE IF WE'RE GOING TO CATCH YOUR LOVELY PRIZE!
I WAS IN LOVE ONCE MYSELF, YOU KNOW. DID I EVER TELL YOU--
SAVE YOUR BREATH, MAYOR...

"...I HAVE NO INTEREST IN YOUR STORIES."
The Next Day
THIS MORNING IS OFF TO AN ADVANTAGEOUS START! WELCOME TO SHEEPSHEAD HARBOR.
YOU KNOW THIS PLACE?

I KNOW IT WELL! IN FACT, THE HARBORMASTER OWES ME A SIZABLE FAVOR. IF I COULD CONVINCE HIM TO PART WITH ONE OF HIS CLIPPERS TO CLEAR HIS DEBT, WE'LL SAVE QUITE A BIT OF TIME ON OUR TREK.
LET US SPEAK WITH HIM, THEN.

OH NO NO NO... LET *ME* HANDLE THE NEGOTIATIONS. YOU WAIT RIGHT HERE. STAY OUT OF TROUBLE, LAD!
VERY WELL.

GOOD DAY MADAM! SUCH LOVELY WARES--
YOU?!? TAKE THEM. TAKE WHATEVER YOU WANT!

GREETINGS, FRIENDS! I'M LOOKING FOR THE HARBORMASTER. WOULD YOU BE SO KIND AS TO DIRECT ME TO HIM?
YER LOOKIN' AT HIM. ANY OF YOU LOT KNOW THIS FANCY DAN?

PISH-POSH. I'M A CONCERNED CITIZEN. LOOK THERE, DOWN THE DOCK! THAT CLOWN IS A **WANTED CRIMINAL**. THERE'S A HANDSOME BOUNTY FOR HIS HIDE.
I'LL BE... IT'S HIM ALRIGHT. **THE DIRTY PIRATE THAT KILLED CAPPY!**
A PIRATE? ERR... YES... POOR, POOR CAPPY...

HE DON'T LOOK LIKE MUCH TO ME.
FIGHT! PLACE YOUR BETS, LADIES AND GENTS...

NO NEED FOR HYSTERICS, M'LADY-- I MEAN YOU NO HARM!
KEEP AWAY FROM ME!

OY.

I BEG YOUR PAR-

WHAM!

DOESN'T ANYONE KNOW HOW TO FIGHT FAIR IN THIS INFERNAL REALM?

HE'S *PUNY*! HARD TO BELIEVE THIS SQUEAKER TOOK OUT HALF THE BOOGEYMAN'S NAVY.
GET 'IM, ANCHOR!

ANOTHER BET FOR MR. ANCHOR! WHO'LL GIVE ME TEN TO ONE ON THE CLOWN? TWENTY TO ONE? ANY TAKERS?
ANCHOR'S GOT IT IN THE BAG!
MY MONEY'S ON ANCHOR!

TIME TO DIE!
RRRAARGH!

I'D LOST TRACK IN ALL OF THE EXCITEMENT.
IS *THAT* WHAT TIME IT IS?
KRUNCH!

GRRR... HOLD STILL!
BLASTED CHAIN... STUCK...

I REALLY MUST BE ON MY WAY. TIME FLIES...

...AND SO MUST I. ALLEY OOP!
PUNT!

TEP!
AH, BUT WHERE ARE MY MANNERS?
THANK YOU FOR THE DANCE...

...AND GOOD NIGHT.
THUNK!

PLEASURE DOING BUSINESS WITH YOU. THANK YOU FOR YOUR MONEY.

WHY AM I NOT SURPRISED?
MAKE WAY, FIGHT'S OVER! NOTHING LEFT TO SEE HERE!

MAYOR!
AH... WELL DONE, LAD. WE MAKE A GREAT TEAM. DON'T YOU THINK?
YOU GAMBLED WITH MY LIFE?!?
SHUNK!
WE NEEDED MONEY TO BUY A SHIP! I KNEW YOU WOULD WIN. I ALSO KNEW YOU WOULDN'T TRUST MY PLAN. BUT LOOK! IT WORKED!
YES... IT WOULD APPEAR SO.
ALTHOUGH THE NEXT TIME YOU FEEL THE NEED TO IMPROVISE, I'D APPRECIATE SOME ADVANCE NOTICE.
OF COURSE...
...NOW LET'S SEE ABOUT A SCHOONER.

OUR COURSE IS SET, JESTER. DUE WEST. WE SHOULD REACH THE SHORES OF THE INDIAN NATION BY DAYBREAK.
I'LL SHOW YOU THE WAY... THAT WAS OUR DEAL. ONCE WE REACH GROUND, YOU'RE ON YOUR OWN.

TO BE THE MASTER OF MY OWN FATE? I WELCOME IT.

NOW. HERE, ON THIS BOAT. THIS IS THE FIRST PEACE I'VE KNOWN SINCE I ENTERED THE DARK. I WILL FIND THE PRINCESS, AND I WILL SHARE THIS FEELING WITH HER.
ALL OF THE FIGHTING. THE COLONEL DYING. MAX AND PERCY JOCKEYING FOR CONTROL. I WANT TO PUT IT BEHIND ME.

HA! HE REALLY HAD THE WOOL PULLED OVER YOUR EYES, EH BOY?
I WANT TO BELIEVE MAX IS TRUE, BUT AFTER WHAT HE DID--
NOT THE BEAR... THE PIG!
THUMP!

WHAT--
SHHHHHH! DID YOU FEEL THAT?
THUMP!

THERE IT IS AGAIN!
ROCKS? PERHAPS WE'VE RUN OFF COURSE?

AHH! SOMETHING FAR WORSE I FEAR!
THUMP! THUMP! THUMP!

WE MUST TURN BACK. JESTER, HELP ME!
WE WILL PRESS ON. THE BOAT CAN WITHSTAND A PATCH OF ROUGH SEA.

I WOULD NOT BE SO SURE, CLOWN!
FWOOOOSH!

SSMMAASSH!
NOOO!
RRROOOOOAAAR!

SPLOOSH!

WHUUF!
SMACK!

KRRRSSSH!

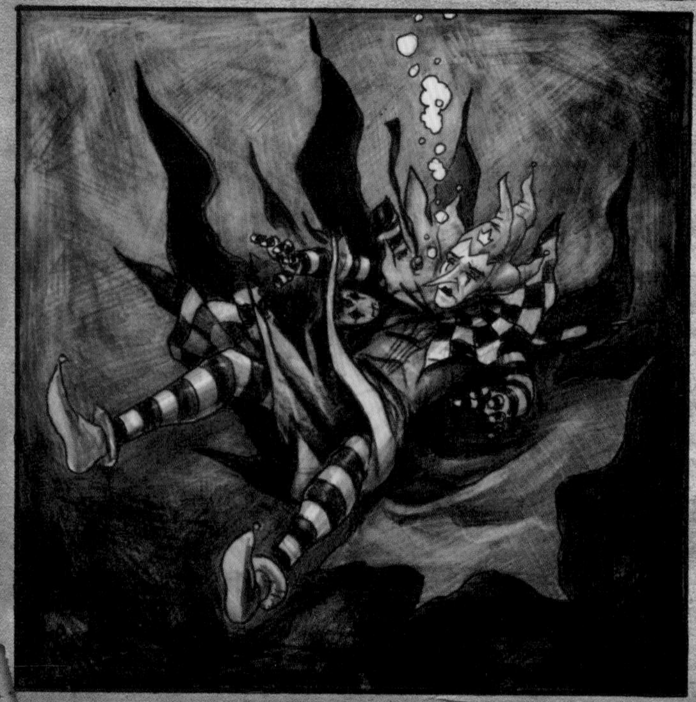

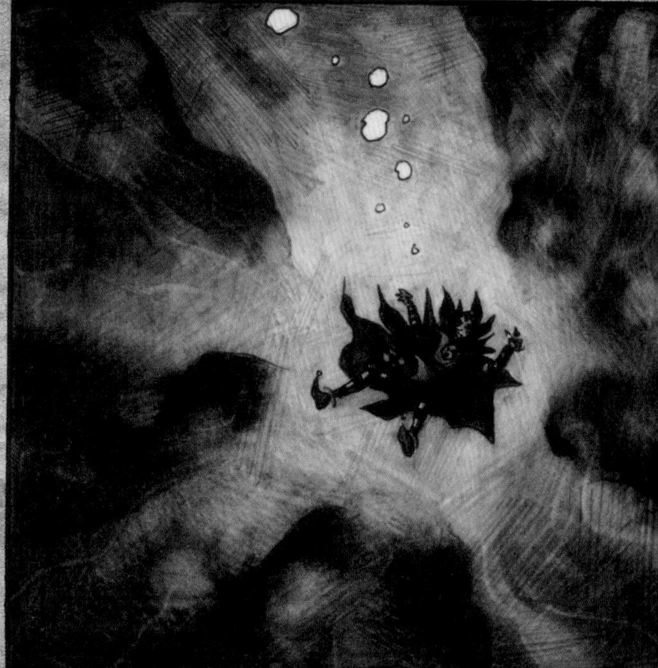

Chapter 2:
Lost Brothers

Before...

ONE FOR YOU...

... AND ONE FOR YOU. ALL THE WAY FROM ENGLAND.

YOU BOYS HAVE FUN WITH THOSE. RUN ALONG, NOW.

GOOD TO SEE THE OLD HOUSE IS STILL STANDING, SIS.

ALICE, YOU ALWAYS SPOIL THEM WHEN YOU RETURN FROM YOUR TRIPS.

HEY! NOT SO FAST, WHAT DO YOU SAY?

OH, RIGHT! THANK YOU, AUNT ALICE!

THANK YOU!

JOHNNY, NO - YOU'RE BREAKING THE SPRING!
HA HA! LOOK!
CUT IT OUT!
NO! THIS ONE'S MINE! LET GO!
MOM!
STOP TWISTING THE-- GREAT. YOU'VE RUINED IT!
YOU BROKE MY TOY!
DID NOT!
BOYS? EVERYTHING OKAY IN THERE?
THAT WAS BRAND NEW! NOW WE'RE BOTH GONNA GET IT. QUICK--

"--HIDE IT IN THE CLOSET."
-KAFF!-
THE STRANGEST DREAM...
MAYOR! DO YOU HAVE ANY IDEA WHERE IN THE DARK WE MIGHT BE?
REGARDLESS, LET'S JUST HOPE THAT THE NATIVES ARE--
THWIP!
WHY, OH WHY ARE THE NATIVES NEVER FRIENDLY?
PLUNK!

YOU'VE CAUGHT ME IN A RATHER UNPLEASANT MOOD.

THWI-THUMP!
THWIP!
THWIP!

AH, THERE YOU ARE.
PREPARE TO RECEIVE A GIFT OF HATCHETS, ARCHER.

STAY BACK!
SOMEBODY, HELP! THE BAD CLOWN IS HERE! HE WANTS TO HURT ME!

IT WAS ***YOUR*** ARROW THAT WOKE MY WRATH.
ACCEPT YOUR PUNISHMENT LIKE A--

WAAAAAAH!
YOU'RE A VERY -SNIFF!- BAD TOY! WAAAH!
CEASE YOUR BLUBBERING, CHILD. I WILL NOT HARM YOU.
YOU'VE GOT THAT RIGHT, VILLAIN.

LADIES!
SWORDS AND SPEARS? HOW VERY UNBECOMING. LOWER YOUR WEAPONS, MY DEARS. SUCH BEHAVIOR BETRAYS YOUR TRUE BEAUTY.
REST ASSURED... I WILL GLADLY FOLLOW WHEREVER YOU MAY LEAD.
WE ARE IMMUNE TO YOUR FLATTERY, KNAVE. SPEAK ANOTHER WORD AND RISK LOSING YOUR TONGUE.
YOU'RE COMING WITH US.

Bakerstown
GAH-- DON'T BREAK ME! **PLEASE!**
TELL ME WHAT I WISH TO KNOW.
BREAD
BAKERY

I AM HUNTING A **BOY**. HIS TRAIL GOES COLD HERE IN THIS VILLAGE.
TH-THERE WERE TWO OF THEM. **PIE THIEVES!** WE CHASED THEM.
TWO BOYS?

MISCHIEVOUS TOYS. THEY JUMPED ON A PASSING TRAIN, HEADING EAST. TOWARDS BROOKLYN CREEK. I SWEAR IT!
IF YOU ARE LYING...

...I WILL RETURN FOR YOUR HEAD.
KRACK!
OWW! THE BOOGEYMAN WILL HEAR OF THIS.
WE ARE EVER LOYAL TO HIS WILL!

THAT IS WHY YOU ARE WEAK. GIVE YOUR MASTER A MESSAGE.
STAY OUT OF MY WAY. SHOULD HE INTERFERE, HE TOO SHALL DIE BY MY HAND.
THIS I SWEAR.
"THE STRANGEST DREAM..."

Elsewhere in the Dark...
...IT HAS TO BE A DREAM. TRAPPED IN THIS PLACE, WITH ALL OF THESE OLD TOYS-- AND THAT THING THAT DRAGGED ME INTO THE CLOSET?
MONSTERS LIKE THAT AREN'T REAL.

BUT WHY CAN'T I WAKE UP?
I WANT TO GO **FASTER**. DON'T JUST STAND THERE, LOAD MORE COAL! AND WHY SHOULD ***YOU*** GET TO PLAY ALL THE TIME? IT'S ***MY TURN*** TO BE THE ENGINEER!

WILL YOU BE QUIET!? I THINK...
I THINK WE'RE BOTH IN TERRIBLE TROUBLE.

WE'RE FINALLY HAVING FUN HERE, SO WHICH IS IT? ARE YOU DREAMING OR NOT? YOU KNOW WHAT? MAYBE THIS IS MY DREAM. DON'T RUIN IT!

NO MORE GAMES! WE DON'T BELONG HERE-- DON'T YOU UNDERSTAND?
THERE HAS TO BE A WAY OUT. WE HAVE TO FIND IT.
PETE, IS THERE ANYPLACE YOU CAN TAKE US? SOME KIND OF DOORWAY THAT LEADS OUT OF YOUR WORLD, AND INTO OURS?
STRANGE QUESTION FOR A TOY. THERE'S A WAY IN, OF COURSE, BUT I'VE NEVER HEARD OF A WAY OUT.
IF ANYBODY HAD AN ANSWER, IT WOULD BE THAT OL' INJUN CHIEF. I SUPPOSE WE COULD ASK HIM...
...BUT IT'LL BE DANGEROUS. THEY DON'T TAKE KINDLY TO VISITORS.
WE'LL HAVE TO RISK IT. IT MIGHT BE OUR ONLY CHANCE.
WELL THEN! YOU TOYS JUST SIT BACK AND ENJOY THE SCENERY.
NEXT STOP... THE INJUN LANDS!

OF COURSE, THE GREAT SEA BEAST WAS NO MATCH FOR ME. AFTER WRESTLING IT INTO SUBMISSION, I BRIEFLY CONSIDERED COOKING HIM, BUT TOOK PITY ON THE GIANT AND SET HIM FREE.
HE HAD A MELANCHOLY ABOUT HIM, AS IF HE CARRIED THE PAIN OF UNREQUITED LOVE.
YOU THINK THE SEA MONSTER WAS IN LOVE?
GIGGLE!
INDEED I DO. FOR I TOO KNOW THAT PAIN... AND I DO NOT JOKE WHEN IT COMES TO MATTERS OF THE HEART!
SUCH A ROMANTIC!
SIGH! WHO'S THE LUCKY TOY?
THAT'S ENOUGH! NEXT YOU'LL BE HANDING HIM YOUR SPEARS AND GIGGLING AS HE RUNS YOU THROUGH!
LITTLE GIRL, I--
LITTLE GIRL, NOTHING. I'M NOT INTERESTED IN YOUR STORIES. IF YOU DON'T PIPE DOWN I'LL TELL YOU ONE OF MY OWN.
IT'S CALLED "HOW I STABBED THE MOUTHY CLOWN WHO WOULDN'T SHUT UP."
CHARMING.
WE'RE HERE.

THAT WAY. REBECCA WILL DECIDE YOUR FATE.

I EXPECTED MUCH MORE OF A FIGHT FROM THE INFAMOUS **LAUGHING GHOST**.
THE "TERROR OF THE SEAS" INDEED. SO MUCH FOR REPUTATIONS.

REBECCA, IS IT?
I HAVEN'T THE SLIGHTEST... BUT I WONDER IF YOU'VE SEEN MY COMPANION? PORTLY CHAP? OVERLY BOASTFUL?
UNFORTUNATELY, YES.

EVEN IN THE STOCKADE HE'S STILL RATHER GRABBY.
HO, HO, JESTER, MY BOY! IT'S PARADISE!

RELEASE HIM AT ONCE.
DO NOT TEST MY PATIENCE. YOU STOLE CARGO FROM THE BOOGEYMAN'S FLEET.
GIVE IT TO ME.

YOU HAVE ME CONFUSED WITH SOMEONE ELSE.
NOW IF YOU'LL EXCUSE ME...
HALT!

YOU'RE NOT GOING ANYWHERE.
OBEY ME, OR PERISH!
NEITHER OF THOSE OPTIONS SPEAKS TO ME.
YOU DON'T MIND IF I BORROW THIS?
THANK YOU, LOVELY.
SCOUNDREL!
IT'S A LITTLE LATE FOR FLATTERY.
CLANG!

FINALLY, YOU SHOW YOUR TRUE COLORS!
MERELY DEFENDING MYSELF, M'LADY.
WOULDN'T YOU RATHER DISCUSS THIS OVER DINNER? I'M ABSOLUTELY FAMISHED.
INSOLENT DOG!
YOUR WORDS WOUND ME, REBECCA.
IF YOU WON'T BUDGE ON DINNER...
...LET'S AT LEAST OFFER YOUR SUBJECTS A SHOW.

OH-HO! YOU'RE REALLY QUITE GRACEFUL, MADAM. LIGHTER THAN AIR!

UNHAND ME, YOU BUFFOON!
BAP!

ON YOUR FEET.
NOT EXACTLY THE REACTION I WAS HOPING FOR.

WHO ARE YOU?
I AM BUT A HUMBLE PILGRIM ON LOVE'S MISSION, M'LADY.

HE CALLED YOU JESTER. THAT NAME IS FAMILIAR TO ME...
...ARE YOU ONE OF THE RENEGADE TOYS THE BOOGEYMAN SEEKS?
AND IF I AM?
THEN YOU STILL MAY PROVE USEFUL.
JESTER, AT YOUR SERVICE.

RELEASE THE FAT ONE. SEE THAT HE KEEPS HIS HANDS TO HIMSELF, LEST I TAKE THEM FROM HIM.
YOU HAVE MY WORD!
SMALL COMFORT IN THAT.

ESCORT THESE TOYS TO OUR GUEST CHAMBERS. HAVE THE SEAMSTRESS FASHION SOME APPROPRIATE CLOTHING FOR THEM BOTH.
I HAVE FURTHER QUESTIONS FOR YOU, JESTER. YOUR PRESENCE IS REQUESTED AT THE PALACE TONIGHT. DO NOT BE LATE.

The Black Forest
WILL SOMEONE PLEASE EXPLAIN WHERE WE'RE HEADED?
SURE LOOKS LIKE SHE'S IGNORING YOU TO ME.
I WILL *NOT* BE IGNORED, ROSE!

I'M SO GLAD THE WALKING HAT-RACK IS AMUSED.
HERE WE ARE, WALKING AIMLESSLY THROUGH ENEMY TERRITORY, AND THE ONLY ***QUALIFIED LEADER*** AMONG US IS BEING KEPT IN THE DARK!

IS THERE NO END TO YOUR COMPLAINING, PERCY? I AM KEEPING YOU SAFE ON THIS FOOL'S ERRAND. THAT IS ALL YOU NEED TO KNOW.

WE WILL CAMP HERE.
HMMPH. THIS HARDLY LOOKS ADEQUATE. I THINK WE SHOULD VOTE.

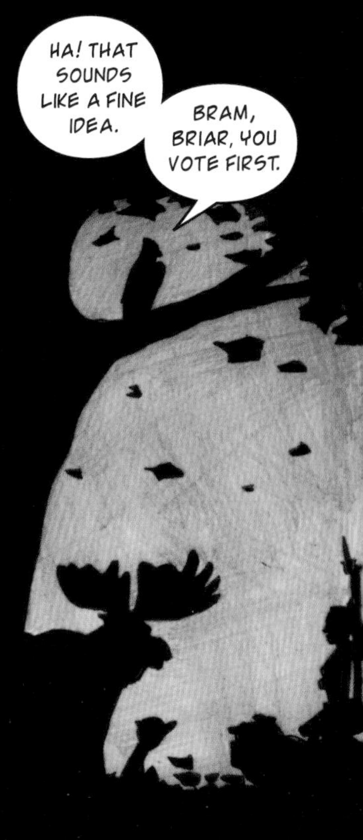
HA! THAT SOUNDS LIKE A FINE IDEA.
BRAM, BRIAR, YOU VOTE FIRST.

I VOTE WE CAMP HERE.
AFTER WE EAT YOUR LIVER.
THERE'S NO NEED FOR THESE SCARE TACTICS...
THAT'S ENOUGH, YOU TWO. KING MAX'S ORDERS ARE TO GET THEM OUT OF THE DARK ALIVE.
BUT SINCE THERE ISN'T ANY WAY OUT...
IF YOU HAVE TO EAT HIM, MAKE SURE ROSE DOESN'T SEE.
BARBARIC!
THIS IS AN OUTRAGE! QUACKERS, DID YOU HEAR HOW THEY THREATENED ME?
YOU DO IT TO YOURSELF, PERCY. WE'D ALL BE DEAD IF IT WASN'T FOR ROSIE COMING TO SAVE US. YOU SHOULD BE THANKING HER.
OR BETTER YET, JUST STOP TALKING FOR A WHILE.

CARE FOR SOME COMPANY, ROSIE?
NO.
AND IT'S ROSE.

LISTEN , I'M SORRY ABOUT PERCY. IT'S HARD TO SEE, BUT HE'S REALLY NOT ALL BAD.

YAWN!
WE USED TO HAVE ALL KINDS OF FUN BACK IN THE BOY'S ROOM. PERCY WAS ALWAYS GOOD FOR A LAUGH. THIS ONE TIME, MAX--
WELL, YOU GET THE PICTURE.

SAY, WHERE ARE WE HEADED ANYWAY?
GET OFF OF ME!

IF YOU MUST KNOW, KING MAX SAYS YOU ENTERED THE DARK AT BROOKLYN CREEK.
THAT'S AS GOOD A PLACE TO--
ZZZZZzZZzZz...

SWELL.
SLEEP TIGHT, DUCK.

Later...
WELL, AREN'T WE LOOKING DAPPER THIS EVENING?
THIS WAY, LAD. LET'S NOT KEEP THE PRETTY LADIES WAITING. I'M FEELING RATHER FRISKY TONIGHT!

WELCOME, GUESTS.
NOW THAT YOU HAVE HAD A CHANCE TO RELAX, WOULD YOU BE SO KIND AS TO TELL ME...

...EXACTLY HOW YOU HAPPENED UPON OUR SHORES?
'TIS A LONG STORY, M'LADY.

I ENTERED THIS REALM WITH SEVERAL OTHER TOYS IN AN EFFORT TO RECLAIM MY MASTER, A HUMAN BOY, FROM THE FOUL CLUTCHES OF THE BOOGEYMAN.
BUT OUR PARTY SOON SPLINTERED--BETRAYED FROM WITHIN.
NOW I SEEK TO RESCUE THAT WHICH WAS STOLEN FROM ME.
MY PRINCESS. THE ONE I LOVE. I BELIEVE THAT SHE IS NOW IN THE INDIAN LANDS.

I KNOW NOTHING ABOUT A BOY. MY MASTER WAS A GIRL. ALICE.
THAT IS JUST ONE OF THE MANY MYSTERIES THAT SURROUNDS YOU, JESTER.
YOU BEAR AN UNCANNY RESEMBLANCE TO THE LAUGHING GHOST, THE SCOURGE OF THE NORTHERN SEAS. HE PATROLS OUR WATERS, PREYING ON ANY WHO CROSS HIS PATH.
THE BOOGEYMAN HAS ALWAYS TOLERATED HIS PRESENCE... UNTIL RECENTLY.
THE GHOST'S ATTACKS HAVE GROWN EVEN MORE FEROCIOUS.
HE HUNTS WITH A RENEWED PURPOSE, EVEN ATTACKING THE BOOGEYMAN'S NAVY IN SEARCH OF HIS PRIZE.
WE ARE LOYAL TO THE BOOGEYMAN'S WILL... WHEN IT IS CONVENIENT. OUR TENUOUS ALLEGIANCE OFFERS GREAT INSIGHT AS TO WHAT TRANSPIRES IN THE DARK.
HE CALLED ON US TO CAPTURE THE LAUGHING GHOST AFTER HIS LATEST RAID. WHATEVER THE GHOST STOLE, IT IS SOMETHING THE BOOGEYMAN DESIRES.
I WANT IT FOR MYSELF.

I WANT NO PART OF THIS. MY PATH LEADS ELSEWHERE, REBECCA.
TO THE INDIAN LANDS? THEY WILL SLAUGHTER YOU BEFORE YOU EVEN GET CLOSE.
YOU INTRIGUE ME, JESTER. I WILL SHOW YOU SAFE PASSAGE, IN EXCHANGE FOR ANY ASSISTANCE YOU CAN PROVIDE ME IN MY QUEST.

MAYOR, THIS DEAL REEKS OF COMPLICATIONS. DO YOU KNOW THE WAY, OR NOT?
OF COURSE! ERR, THAT IS TO SAY...
NO.
BLAST.

I OFFER MYSELF AS PAYMENT IN EXCHANGE FOR SAFE PASSAGE. I WILL MAKE THIS GRUELING SACRIFICE AND STAY BEHIND, SO THAT MY DEAR FRIEND MAY CONTINUE HIS QUEST.
USE ME HOWEVER YOU SEE FIT.
I ACCEPT.
EXCELLENT. I WILL MAKE ALL OF THE NECESSARY PREPARATIONS-- BUT FOR NOW, EAT, DRINK, AND ENJOY YOURSELVES. YOU HAVE THE FULL HOSPITALITY OF THE DOLL NATION.

A PARTY? I SUGGEST YOU ALL GET YOUR REST.
WE LEAVE AT DAWN.

ZZZZZZZZZZ...
SNORT!
MORNING ALREADY?

I SHOULD THANK YOU, DUCK. YOUR SNORING KEPT ME FROM FALLING ASLEEP.
IT IS ONLY DUE TO YOUR ANNOYANCE THAT I WAS ABLE TO STAND GUARD.
MY PLEASURE!

HEAR THAT, PERCY? I'M IMPORTANT. NYAAAH!
GROAN! THAT WAS AN INSULT, YOU LOVESICK FEATHER BRAIN.
SNAP!

WAITAMINNIT-- SOMEONE'S THERE.

JESTER...
...IS THAT YOU?

Chapter 3:
Diplomatic Dilemmas

TOOT TOOT
WE ARE NOW ENTERING THE SCRAP YARD.
A GHOULISH PLACE, IF YOU ASK ME. NOT SOMEPLACE I'D RECOMMEND FREQUENTING.
IT'S HORRIBLE, BESSIE.
ALL OF THESE TOYS WERE BROKEN HERE? HOW DID THIS HAPPEN?
BESSIE

MOSTLY DURING THE BOOGEYMAN'S WARS. SOME JUST FOR HIS PLAIN OL'AMUSEMENT. NO MATTER HOW FREE WE MAY THINK WE ARE OUR TIME ON THE RAILS IS RARELY OUR OWN.
I... I NEVER THOUGHT ABOUT IT THAT WAY.
BOO-HOO. TOYS ARE MADE FOR PEOPLE TO PLAY WITH. SOMETIMES THEY GET BROKEN.

WE WERE NEVER PLAYED WITH. NEVER EVEN OPENED, JUST PUT IN THE CLOSET FOR A LATER DAY THAT NEVER CAME. THE DARK IS ALL SAM, BESSIE AND ME KNOW.
I NEVER PLAYED WITH TRAINS MUCH. I'M SORRY.
DON'TAPOLOGIZE! IN HERE OUR TRACKS ARE SPREAD WIDE AND WE CAN STEAM OFF ANYWHERE.
UNFORTUNATELY, FROM TIME TO TIME WE ARE TASKED WITH DOING THE BOOGEYMAN'S BIDDING. IN THOSE CASES WE--

SPEAK OF THE DEVIL, MR. CONDUCTOR, AND HE SHALL APPEAR.
HUSH. THEY'LL HEAR YOU, BESSIE. YOU DON'T WANT TO END UP HERE, D'YA? NOW SLOW US DOWN.

ARE WE IN DANGER, MR. CONDUCTOR?
ARE YOU KIDDING? THE WHOLE PLACE IS LOOKING FOR US! WE NEED TO HIDE!

IN THE NAME OF THE BOOGEYMAN, STOP THAT TRAIN!
IT'S ABOUT TIME ONE'A THESE ENGINES CAME BY. THIS SCRAP YARD'S GIVIN' ME THE CREEPS.
BESSIE

WE CLAIM THIS TRAIN IN THE NAME OF THE BOOGEYMAN'S ARMY.
HOW MANY OF YA ARE THERE ONBOARD?

JUST US TWO AND OL' BESSIE, OF COURSE.
BESSIE?

OUR STEAM ENGINE. THAT'S HER NAME.
DON'T PLAY SMART WITH ME, OLD MAN.
YOU WERE SUPPOSED TO GET HERE DAYS AGO.

WE HEARD NOTHING OF ANY CARGO PICK UP HERE. YOU MUST BE WAITING ON ANOTHER TRAIN.

WE'D LOVE TO HELP BUT WE WERE TASKED WITH ROUNDING UP SOME DELICATE ITEMS IN THE INDIAN LANDS. WE DON'T HAVE TIME TO DIVERT OUR ROUTE SO--

DON'T TELL ME MY BUSINESS!

THE BOOGEYMAN'S NAVY WAS DEALT A NASTY BLOW BY THE LAUGHING GHOST. THIS ARMY HAS BEEN ASSEMBLED TO GET REVENGE AND WE AIM TO HAVE IT.

THERE'S RUMORS THE GHOST'S SHIP HAS BEEN SEEN SAILING ALONG THE COASTLINE. IF WE'RE LUCKY, WE CAN HEAD HIM OFF IN THE INJUN LANDS.

PROBABLY BE OUR BEST SHOT AT HIM.

The Black Forest
UH, GUYS! THIS AIN'T OUR JESTER!
WHO ARE YOU?
HE'S HUMAN...
...THAT MEANS HE'S WITH THE BOOGEYMAN!

SMACK
WAITAMIN-ACK!
SILENCE!

I AM THE ***LAUGHING GHOST*** AND I OWE MY ALLEGIANCE TO NO MAN OR BEAST.

DECLARING ME AN AGENT OF THE BOOGEYMAN HAS EARNED YOU NOTHING BUT A SWIFT DEATH. PREPARE TO BE BROKEN.

BRAM! BRIAR! STOP HIM!
GET THOSE GUNS!

YOU WANT MY GUNS!? YOU SHALL RECEIVE THEM!
RAAH!
DISARM THE FRIGHTENING MAN, BROTHER!

FOR GOODNESS SAKE LET HIM PASS! WE DON'T EVEN KNOW IF HE MEANS US HARM!
YOU'RE GOING TO GET US ALL KILLED!

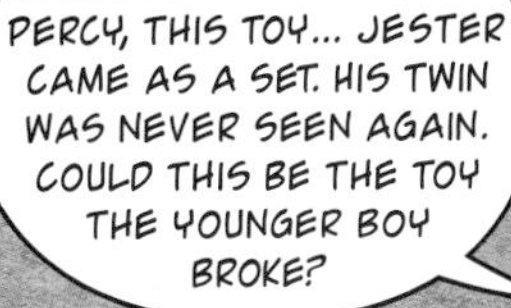

PERCY, THIS TOY... JESTER CAME AS A SET. HIS TWIN WAS NEVER SEEN AGAIN. COULD THIS BE THE TOY THE YOUNGER BOY BROKE?
I DON'T CARE WHAT HAPPENED TO HIM! WHY CAN DIPLOMACY NEVER RULE THE DAY?

YIIP!
RRRRRRR.
THE ONLY DIPLOMACY IN THE DARK--

OOF!
--COMES AT THE END OF A GUN.

YOU BLEED A LOT FOR A GHOST.
YES, WELL--

--YOU TALK A LOT FOR A MOOSE.
BLAM!

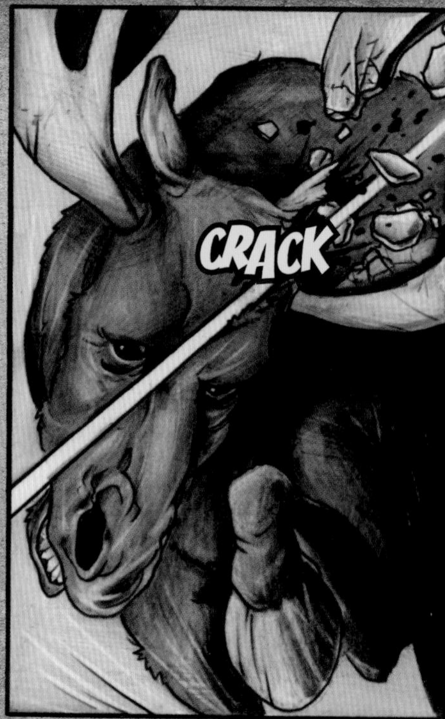
CRACK

YOUR MOUTH GAVE AWAY ANY CHANCE YOU HAD OF DEFEATING ME, FOOL!
THUD!

WAIT! I WANTED TO LET YOU PASS! AND I AM SO SORRY ABOUT YOU BEING BROKEN. I UNDERSTAND YOUR PAIN. PLEASE, LEAVE ME ALONE.

IF YOU ARE PLANNING ON WHIMPERING ME TO DEATH...

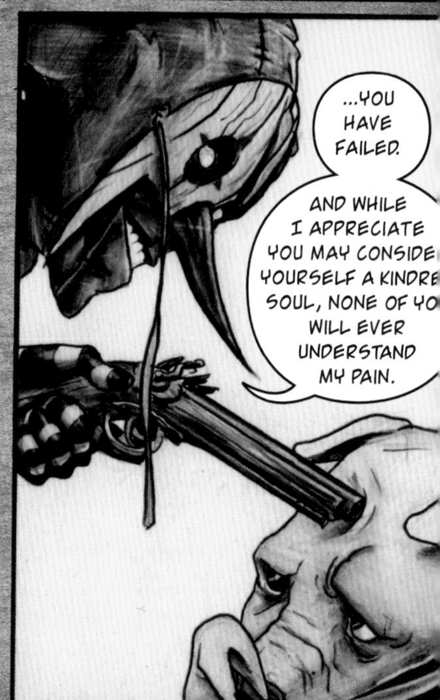
...YOU HAVE FAILED.
AND WHILE I APPRECIATE YOU MAY CONSIDE YOURSELF A KINDRE SOUL, NONE OF YO WILL EVER UNDERSTAND MY PAIN.

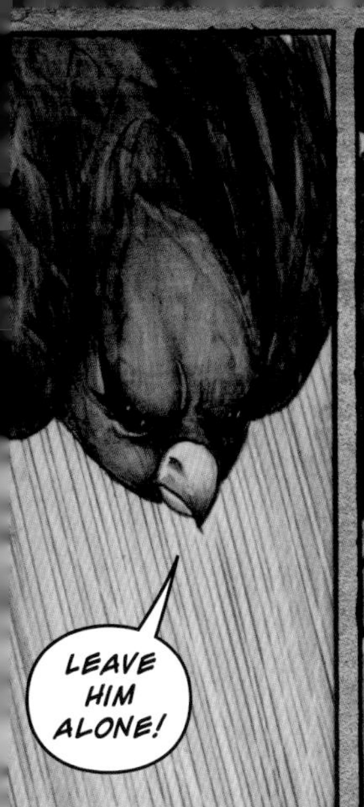
LEAVE HIM ALONE!

ARRRHH!
SLASH!
EVERYONE! NOW WHILE HE'S DISTRACTED!
DIZZY...BUT I'M WIT'YOU ROSIE.

YOU! YOU DARE REMOVE MY MASK!
YOU THINK SCARRING ME FURTHER WILL STOP ME? YOU WILL FEEL PAIN FOR THAT, BIRD!

SNAP!
AIIIEEEE!

I CAN'T TAKE IT! NOT ANYMORE!
PERCY, WAIT! COME BACK! WE NEED YOU!
I JUST WANT TO BE LEFT ALONE!

IF YOU ARE COUNTING ON THE PIG FOR HELP, YOU ARE ALREADY LOST.
WHO IS NEXT?
ROSIE? NO...

RRAAH!

OUR FIRST VOLUNTEER. GOODBYE.
BLAM!
YIIP!

THWACK!
STOP IT! I WON'T LET YOU HURT THEM!
DUCK--

--YOU DON'T HAVE A CHOICE IN THE MATTER!
OOF

BLAM!
STEP AWAY FROM THEM.

NOW.
THAT WAS MY FIRST TIME FIRING A GUN, BUT I'M A QUICK STUDY. I PROMISE YOU MY NEXT SHOT WILL BE BETTER.

YOUR EYES TELL ME YOU ARE NO KILLER AND THAT I COULD STILL WIN THE DAY.
DO NOT MISTAKE COMPASSION FOR WEAKNESS. I WILL DO ANYTHING TO PROTECT MY FAMILY.

YOU THINK YOUR FAMILY IS YOUR STRENGTH, BUT IT WILL BE YOUR UNDOING.
YOU ARE LUCKY MY TRUE DESTINY LIES ELSEWHERE.

AROOOO!
NOTHING WILL STOP ME FROM PUNISHING THOSE WHO RUINED ME.
THE BOY AND THE BOOGEYMAN WILL PAY FOR ALL THEY HAVE DONE.

Sunrise in The Doll Kingdom...
...I WIN... I WIN...
...HAPPY DAY... AND NOW TO SEAL MY VICTORY... WITH A KISS... FROM ALL OF YOU...
ASTOUNDING, FILMORE, EVEN YOUR DREAMS FIND A WAY TO BE OFFENSIVE... YOU ARE LUCKY REBECCA AND THE OTHERS ARE NOT PRESENT TO HEAR YOU.
FILMORE, WAKE UP. YOU HAVE SLUMBERED LONG ENOUGH. TODAY WE RETRIEVE THE PRINCESS.
>YAWN< ...YOUR QUEST HAS PERFORATED MY THOUGHTS, MY FRIEND.
I FOUND MYSELF PLAYING A FINE GAME OF CHANCE SURROUNDED BY THE VERY SWEET DOLLS WHO, OF COURSE, ONLY YESTERDAY WANTED TO KILL US.
IN MY DREAM THEY OFFERED A KISS ON THE CHEEK.
SWEET REBECCA WAS FIRST IN LINE TO--
I'M AFRAID THERE IS VERY LITTLE THAT IS SWEET ABOUT OUR HOSTESS. YOU ARE AN EXPERT IN GAMES. WHAT DO YOU THINK HER ANGLE IS?

DO YOU THINK SHE IS TELLING US THE TRUTH? OR IS SHE PLAYING ME FOR THE FOOL I APPEAR TO BE?
YOU ARE MOST LIKELY CORRECT TO BE NERVOUS ABOUT HER.
SHE IS A MYSTERY TO ME, BUT THE FACT THAT SHE HAS HER OWN KINGDOM, SEEMINGLY UNTOUCHED BY THE BOOGEYMAN AND HIS FORCES, LEADS ME TO BELIEVE SHE IS QUITE FORMIDABLE.
OR HIGHLY FAVORED. PROBABLY BOTH.
ARE YOU TELLING ME SHE WORKS FOR THE BOOGEYMAN? THAT SHE IS NOT TRUSTWORTHY?
I AM ONLY CERTAIN OF ONE THING. SHE IS OUR BEST CHANCE TO FIND THE PRINCESS. BEYOND THAT I DO NOT KNOW.
SURVIVAL IN THIS REALM IS NOT ALWAYS A MATTER OF BRUTE STRENGTH OR BATTLE SAVVY. IT IS A MATTER OF GUILE AND DECEIT.
YOU WOULD DO WELL TO REMEMBER THAT SINCE YOUR HEART IS ALWAYS AFFIXED SQUARELY TO YOUR SLEEVE. HIDING YOUR BELIEFS IS NOT A CHOICE, HERE IT IS A NECESSITY.
HOW DO YOU THINK I HAVE FOUND A WAY TO SURVIVE FOR SO LONG?

SO EAGER TO FIND HIS DEAR, DEAR PRINCESS. I WONDER HOW BROKEN HIS HEART WILL BE IF SHE DOES NOT WANT HIM IN RETURN.
SUCH MUSINGS, SWEET REBECCA... DO I HEAR A TWINGE OF REMORSE IN YOUR VOICE?
YOU CHOSE TO KEEP YOUR DOLLS AWAY FROM THE OTHER TOYS FOR JUST SUCH A REASON. THE PAIN OF LOVE WAS TOO MUCH TO BEAR, REMEMBER?
WHAT CAN I DO FOR YOU? I DID NOT EXPECT A VISIT TODAY. HAVE I DONE SOMETHING TO DISPLEASE YOU?
NO, I ONLY DESIRE AN ANSWER FROM OUR LAST CONVERSATION.
THE LAUGHING GHOST HAS TAKEN SOMETHING FROM ME. I NEED IT BACK. HE HAS BEEN SPOTTED MOVING ALONG THE COAST IN HIS SHIP. SOME OF MY TROOPS ARE AFTER HIM, BUT I FEAR THEY WILL FAIL.
YOU AND YOUR WARRIORS WILL FIND HIM AND RETRIEVE IT. FOR THAT YOU WILL BE REWARDED HANDSOMELY.
DO THIS AND I MAY EVEN ALLOW THAT CLOWN YOU ADMIRE TO LIVE.
HOWEVER, IF YOU WISH TO RECONSIDER MY ORIGINAL OFFER, YOU ONLY HAVE TO SAY THE WORD.
MY ANSWER STANDS...

"VERY WELL, REBECCA, BUT REMEMBER. IT IS ONLY BECAUSE I CARE FOR YOU SO MUCH THAT I ALLOW THIS ARRANGEMENT."
"DO NOT MAKE ME REGRET MY DECISION."

AH, THE BEAUTIFUL REBECCA GRACES US WITH HER PRESENCE. YOU ARE A VISION OF--
ENOUGH. WE LEAVE NOW.

IT IS ABOUT TIME. I GROW WEARY OF THESE DELAYS.
I HAVE HALF A MIND TO GIVE YOU A DINGHY AND SEND YOU OFF ON YOUR OWN. WHAT YOU ASK IS NO SMALL TASK.

YOUR FOOLISH HEART IS PROBABLY GOING TO GET US ALL KILLED.
WHAT DID I DO?
WHAT HAVE YOU NOT DONE, MY FRIEND? I LOST A TOWNSHIP TO YOUR FOOLISHNESS...

CURLY, TELL THE CREW TO BE ON THE LOOKOUT. THE LAUGHING GHOST IS OUT THERE SOMEWHERE. HE IS OUR REAL TARGET.
BE DISCREET. WE CAN ILL AFFORD ANY MISSTEPS.
OF COURSE, M'LADY. WE ARE ALL WITH YOU.

"LET'S HOPE I HAVE NOT LED US ALL TO OUR DOOM."
STILL NOTHING. WHERE COULD HE BE HIDING?
REBECCA, A WORD IF I MAY? HOW LONG UNTIL WE ARRIVE AT--
REBECCA WILL CALL FOR YOU IF SHE WISHES TO CONVERSE. BACK TO YOUR--
LADIES, LET HIM PASS AND GIVE US A MOMENT.
I APOLOGIZE. THEY TAKE THEIR JOBS VERY SERIOUSLY.
AS THEY SHOULD. YOU HAVE DONE WELL BY THEM.
SOMETIMES I FEAR I MAY NOT ALWAYS DO WHAT'S RIGHT... THAT I HAVE LED THEM ASTRAY.
FROM WHAT I'VE SEEN OF THIS MAD WORLD, YOU TREAT YOURSELF TOO HARSHLY. YOU HAVE A PLACE THAT IS NOT FILLED WITH HATRED, LIES AND DEATH.
A PLACE UNTOUCHED BY THE BOOGEYMAN. YOU SHOULD BE APPLAUDED.

YES... WELL, WHAT ABOUT YOU? YOU ARE HERE YET YOU STILL BELIEVE IN LOVE.
IS THIS PRINCESS WORTH IT?

YOU WOULD NOT ASK IF YOU HAD MET HER.
SHE IS A KINDRED SPIRIT. STRONG WILLED. A TRUE WARRIOR.

AND YET WHERE SHE IS ONLY THE BOOGEYMAN KNOWS, AND I AM HERE.
SHE WAS NOT WELL. SHE MUST HAVE BEEN TRICKED INTO LEAVING.
TRICKED? I THOUGHT SHE WAS PERFECT?

I SAY! HOW MUCH LONGER UNTIL WE GET THERE?
OH, THANK GOODNESS FOR YOU, FILMORE. FOR ONCE.

THE SEA-- IS GETTING-- A TAD ROUGH! I'M AFRAID-- I MAY BE--SICK!
DOES EVEN HE DESERVE SUCH TREATMENT?
OUR ONLY OTHER OPTION WAS TO REMOVE HIS ROAMING HANDS COMPLETELY.

POINT TAKEN.
BESIDES, OUR JOURNEY IS AT AN END.

JESTER, I GIVE YOU THE INDIAN LANDS.
'TIS AMAZING!
YES, WELL, LET US HOPE IT IS NOT THE LAST LAND OUR EYES SHALL SEE.
OH, WHAT NOW... I PROMISE TO DO GOOD FROM NOW ON... JUST, PLEASE DON'T HIT A TOTEM POLE...

SLOW DOWN, JESTER. AS I'VE TOLD YOU, WE MUST TREAD CAREFULLY. THERE ARE DIPLOMATIC PATHS WE MUST EXPLORE BEFORE--
WE ARE THE WRONGED PARTY HERE. CLEARLY ARTIC STOLE THE PRINCESS FROM US. NOT THE OTHER WAY AROUND.
I TOLD YOU WE WERE GOING TO NEED MORE GALS! SIGNAL THE BOAT.
IT LOOKS AS IF DIPLOMACY MAY BE DELIVERED AT THE END OF A SPEAR, MY DEAR...
...I DON'T SUPPOSED WE COULD CONVINCE THEM WE COME IN PEACE?
SPEAK FOR YOURSELF, FILMORE. PRINCESS, COME OUT!
ARTIC, WHAT HAVE YOU DONE WITH HER? SHOW YOURSELF, THIEF!
OH, THIS IS GOING TO GO SWIMMINGLY.
HISSSS!
THERE YOU ARE! WHERE IS THE PRINCESS? WHAT HAVE YOU DONE WITH HER?
YOU DARE MAKE DEMANDS HERE?! THIS IS OUR TERRITORY.
YOU MADE YOUR CHOICE IN THE JUNGLE WHEN YOU LEFT HER BEHIND TO DIE. I COULD WAIT NO LONGER FOR YOU TO RETURN.
THAT... THAT IS NOT HOW IT HAPPENED! I CAME RIGHT BACK. YOU STOLE HER AWAY! I TRUSTED YOU!

YOU TRUSTED ME TO CARE FOR HER AND I HAVE. FROM WHAT I'VE HEARD OF YOU, IT'S POSSIBLY THE SMARTEST THING YOU HAVE EVER DONE.
SHE IS SAFE HERE. NOT ONLY FROM YOUR SILLY QUEST TO SAVE THE BOY, BUT YOUR BUFFOONERY.
TAKE SOLACE IN THAT. NOW LEAVE BEFORE WE ARE FORCED TO REMOVE YOU.
YOU ARE A COWARD AND A THIEF. NOW STEP ASIDE AND LET ME SEE HER.
OH BOY...
HUSH!

ENOUGH! YOU DARE DISHONOR ME ON THE SHORES OF MY HOME?
I AM GRAND PROTECTOR OF ALL WE HAVE BUILT HERE. YOU WILL PAY FOR YOUR DISRESPECT.

THERE IS NO INSULT IN THE TRUTH. I WILL MAKE THIS QUICK FOR YOU.
THEN I WILL SEE MY PRINCESS.

SHE IS OURS! AND YOU WILL NEVER SEE HER AGAIN!
THIS I SWEAR!
YOU KNOW YOUR CAUSE IS UNJUST. YOUR ANGER MAKES YOU FLAIL ABOUT.
UHH.
I JUST REALIZED THIS MEANS THE PRINCESS IS STILL ALIVE. I WAS SO AFRAID THAT--
I BELIEVE YOU SHOULD CONCERN YOURSELF WITH THE MATTER AT HAND. POST HASTE!

DEVIL! YOU SHALL NOT TAKE HER!

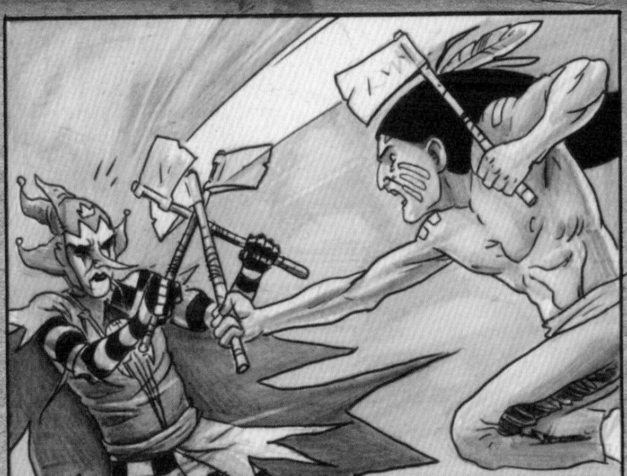

SHE IS NOT A PRIZE TO BE WON OR LOST.

SHE WILL MAKE HER OWN CHOICE...

...BUT WE BOTH KNOW SHE WILL CHOOSE ME!
WHACK!

NOW--

--RELENT! I WANT ONLY TO SPEAK WITH HER. ARE YOU SO FRIGHTENED OF THE TRUTH THAT YOU WILL PREVENT EVEN THAT?

STEP ASIDE! I HAVE BESTED YOUR CHAMPION!
I HAVE EARNED THE RIGHT TO ENTER. I WILL SAY MY PIECE TO THE PRINCESS.
JESTER, BEHIND YOU!
...WHAT HAVE YOU DONE?
JESTER...

I... PLEASE, LET ME EXPLAIN.
DO NOT APPROACH THE PRINCESS, MURDERER.

IT WAS AN ACCIDENT. I SWEAR TO YOU.
ENOUGH! WE CAME HERE IN PEACE. IS THIS HOW YOU WELCOME CIVILIZED GUESTS, PRINCESS?
HISS!

THA-BOOOM!

IT'S THE GHOST!
NO... MY GIRLS...
I WAS SUCH A FOOL... SO DISTRACTED. I LET HIM SNEAK IN BEHIND US.
WHO? JESTER, IS THIS YOUR DOING?
NO. OF COURSE NOT. I WOULD NEVER--
--DO SUCH A THING...
OR WOULD I? IS THAT ME?
HELLO, BROTHER!
SO GOOD OF YOU TO FINALLY JOIN ME IN THE DARK.
WE ARE GOING TO HAVE SUCH FUN TOGETHER.

Chapter 4:
The End of the Line

I ALWAYS KNEW OUR PATHS WOULD CROSS AGAIN.
ALL OF YOU -- COME AND RECEIVE YOUR GIFT OF PAIN!
HA HA HA HA!

READY YOURSELVES, SISTERS-- THIS FIGHT WILL NOT BE EASY. JESTER, CAN WE STILL COUNT ON YOUR BLADES?
THE TOY... FROM MY DREAM...
ENOUGH!

YOU BRING ONLY DEATH TO THE INDIAN NATION, WITH THE PROMISE OF MORE TO COME.

BRAVES, GO AND MEET THE LAUGHING GHOST. DO NOT LET HIM REACH THE SHORE.
PRINCESS- YOU MUST LET ME EXPLAIN.
YOU WASTE YOUR BREATH, JESTER.

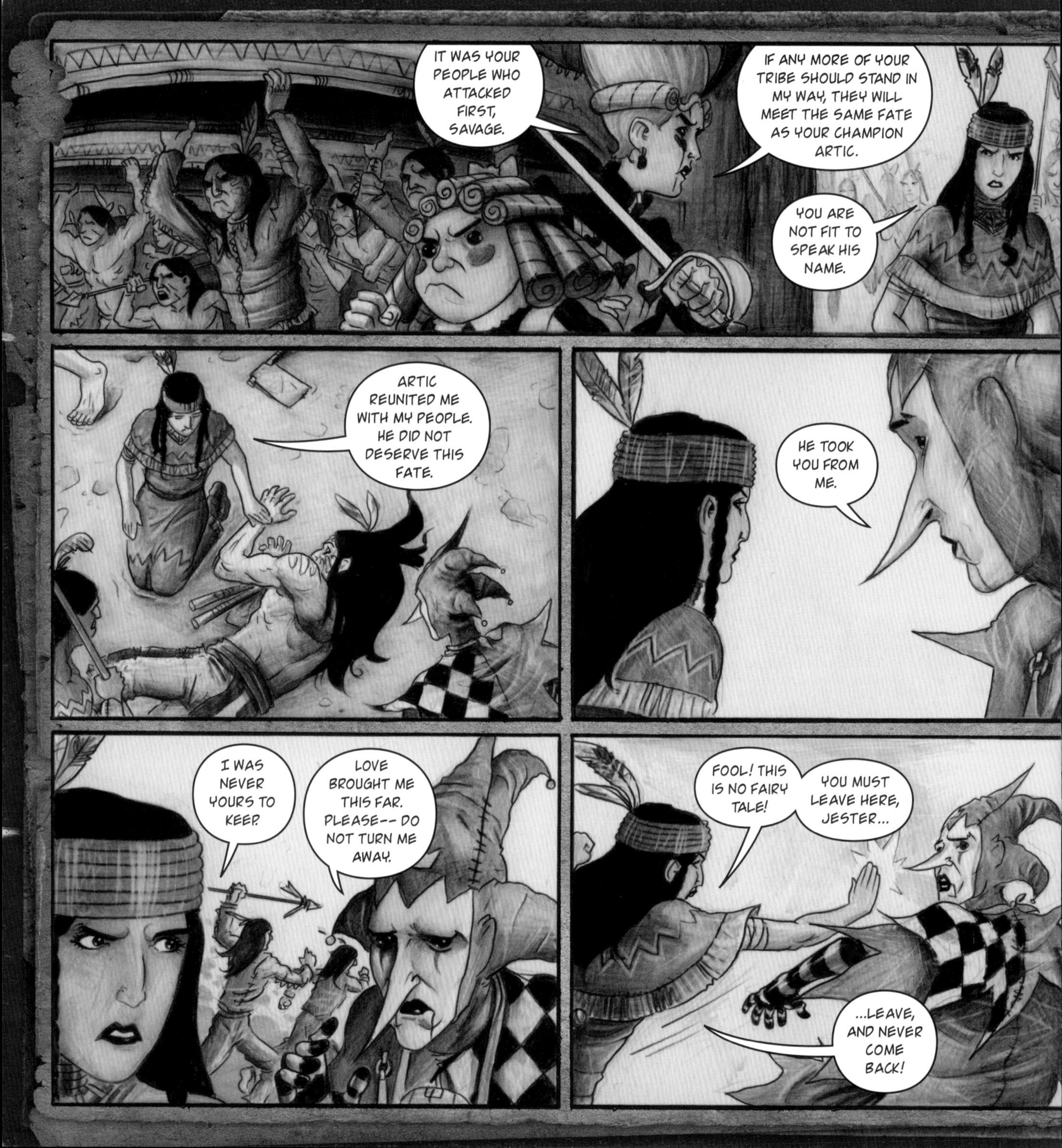
IT WAS YOUR PEOPLE WHO ATTACKED FIRST, SAVAGE.
IF ANY MORE OF YOUR TRIBE SHOULD STAND IN MY WAY, THEY WILL MEET THE SAME FATE AS YOUR CHAMPION ARTIC.
YOU ARE NOT FIT TO SPEAK HIS NAME.
ARTIC REUNITED ME WITH MY PEOPLE. HE DID NOT DESERVE THIS FATE.
HE TOOK YOU FROM ME.
I WAS NEVER YOURS TO KEEP.
LOVE BROUGHT ME THIS FAR. PLEASE-- DO NOT TURN ME AWAY.
FOOL! THIS IS NO FAIRY TALE!
YOU MUST LEAVE HERE, JESTER...
...LEAVE, AND NEVER COME BACK!

TEN LITTLE INJUNS STANDING IN A LINE.

ONE TODDLED HOME...

...AND THEN THERE WERE NINE!
BANG!

NINE LITTLE INJUNS SWINGING ON A GATE!

ONE TUMBLED OFF...
...AND THEN THERE WERE EIGHT!
BANG!

ARTIC DIED BY YOUR HAND. FROM THIS DAY FORTH YOU ARE AN ENEMY OF THE TRIBE.

THIS IS NOT THE WAY OUR STORY ENDS.

GET BACK!
WHAM!

IT IS THE ONLY WAY IT COULD END.
GOODBYE, JESTER.

SLAM!

TIME TO LEAVE, LAD. CONCERN YOURSELF WITH HEARTBREAK LATER, PREFERABLY AT A MUCH SAFER LOCATION.
THIS IS NOT OUR FIGHT.
ON THE CONTRARY, MAYOR...
...IT SEEMS THAT ALL BATTLES ARE MY BURDEN HERE IN THE DARK.
THE INDIANS WILL KILL ME IF I STAY, BUT IT WILL SURELY KILL ME TO LEAVE. THOUGH IT FEELS LIKE THE FINAL ACT, I'M LEFT WONDERING STILL. IS MY TALE A TRAGEDY... OR HIGH COMEDY?
YOU HAVE PROVEN YOURSELF TO BE A LOYAL AND GOOD FRIEND, FILMORE.
I WILL NOT LET YOU DIE ON THIS BEACH.
NO ONE HAS EVER CALLED ME THAT BEFORE.
YOU HAVE EARNED IT.
NOW LET US LEARN WHAT ROLE THE LAUGHING GHOST PLAYS IN THIS GRAND PRODUCTION.

PROTECT THE GATE. NO ONE GETS IN UNTIL THE GHOST IS DEAD.

YES, PRINCESS.
I MUST SPEAK WITH THE ELDER AT ONCE.

IS THIS THE COMING DARKNESS YOU PROPHESIZED, SHAMAN? THE ONE CALLED THE LAUGHING GHOST?
NO, PRINCESS.

THE GREATEST EVIL OF ALL STILL APPROACHES. YOU WILL BE THE ONE TO LEAD US AGAINST HIM, BUT NOT THIS DAY.

TODAY HE HIDES.

GRAOWR! OUT OF MY WAY-- THE GHOST IS MINE!

BOASTFUL BEAST.
KRACK!
THUD!

NO WOUND CAN MATCH THE SUFFERING I HAVE ENDURED!

CURLY!
BLAM!

BLAM!
I WILL TEST THAT STATEMENT, MONSTER.
ALLOW ME TO ADD TO YOUR MISERY!
KLANG!

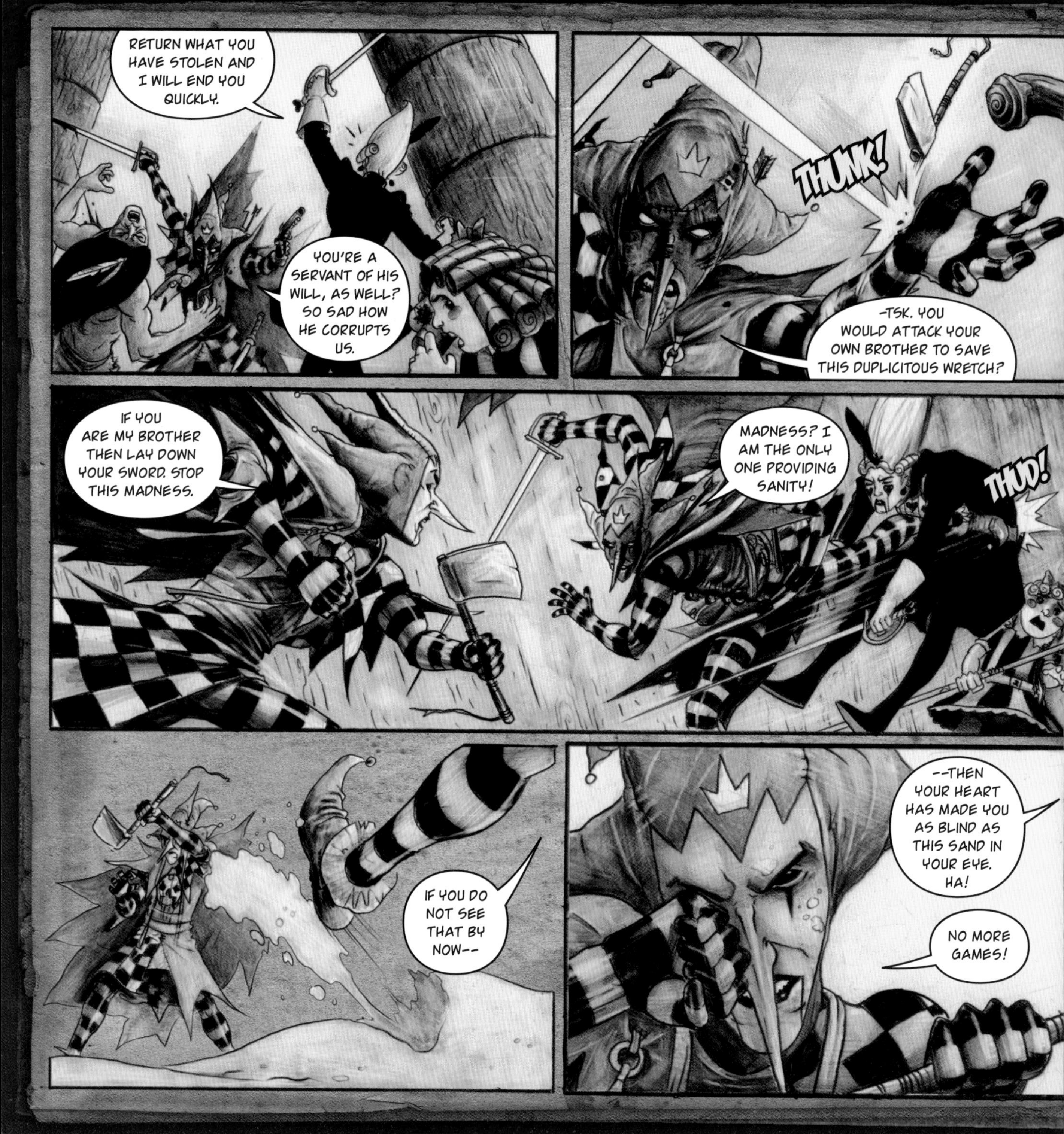
RETURN WHAT YOU HAVE STOLEN AND I WILL END YOU QUICKLY.
YOU'RE A SERVANT OF HIS WILL, AS WELL? SO SAD HOW HE CORRUPTS US.
THUNK!
-TSK. YOU WOULD ATTACK YOUR OWN BROTHER TO SAVE THIS DUPLICITOUS WRETCH?
IF YOU ARE MY BROTHER THEN LAY DOWN YOUR SWORD. STOP THIS MADNESS.
MADNESS? I AM THE ONLY ONE PROVIDING SANITY!
THUD!
IF YOU DO NOT SEE THAT BY NOW--
--THEN YOUR HEART HAS MADE YOU AS BLIND AS THIS SAND IN YOUR EYE. HA!
NO MORE GAMES!

NOT HAVING FUN?
I CAN SEE WHY.

IT'S NOT A PARTY WITHOUT FAVORS!
SNAP

THIS ONE IS FOR YOUR FRIENDS. I DO HOPE THEY FIND IT FESTIVE.
FSSSSSHHHHHH!

HA HA! BE QUICK, BROTHER! TICK-TICK--

BOOM!

DID YOU HEAR THAT?
LOOK! SMOKE, JUST UP AHEAD!
GREAT. WE DON'T NEED ANY MORE TROUBLE. IF THEY CATCH US HIDING HERE--
SHHH! SOMEONE'S COMING!
THAT EXPLOSION... THE LAUGHING GHOST IS ALREADY WAITING FOR US. I'D STAKE MY LIFE ON IT!

BESSIE

GET READY TO FIGHT THE SECOND WE ARRIVE AT THE INDIAN CAMP.

YOU LOT, SPREAD THE WORD. ORDERS'RE TO KILL THE GHOST ON SIGHT AND RETRIEVE THE BOOGEYMAN'S CARGO.
HIS WILL IS THE WAY!

NEVER LET IT BE SAID THAT I DON'T KNOW HOW TO MAKE AN ENTRANCE!
NOW I THINK I'D LIKE TO DANCE WITH YOUR PRINCESS.

MANIAC! STOP THIS SENSELESS VIOLENCE!

HO-HO! STOP?
I'VE BARELY BEGUN.

BOOOOM!
BESSIE

IT'S THE GHOST. TEAR 'IM APART, BOYS! FOR THE GLORY OF THE BOOGEYMAN!
REPEL THE INVADERS! WE ARE A FREE PEOPLE. ANSWER THEIR TYRANNY WITH YOUR SPEARS!
WHAT ARE YOU DOING? IT'S NOT SAFE OUT HERE!
HA HA HA!
THE MORE THE MERRIER!
GET DOWN BEFORE THEY SEE YOU!
METHINKS THE TIME FOR A HASTY DEPARTURE IS NIGH!

YOU THERE. STEP ASIDE! I DEMAND TO SEE YOUR OPERATOR'S LICENSE!
ERR... AIN'T GOT NO LICENSE.
FOR SHAME, SIR.
YOU'VE LEFT ME NO CHOICE BUT TO IMPOUND YOUR VEHICLE.
BUT WHAT ABOUT US?
I RATHER THINK YOU SHOULD FIND A SAFE PLACE TO HIDE.
JESTER! ALL ABOARD, MY BOY!
FILMORE?
PLANNING ON LEAVING SO SOON, BROTHER?
WE STILL HAVE SO MUCH CATCHING UP TO--
AT LAST.
AT LAST!
VENGEANCE WILL BE MINE!
GUN HIM DOWN! DON'T LET THAT CLOWN ESCAPE!

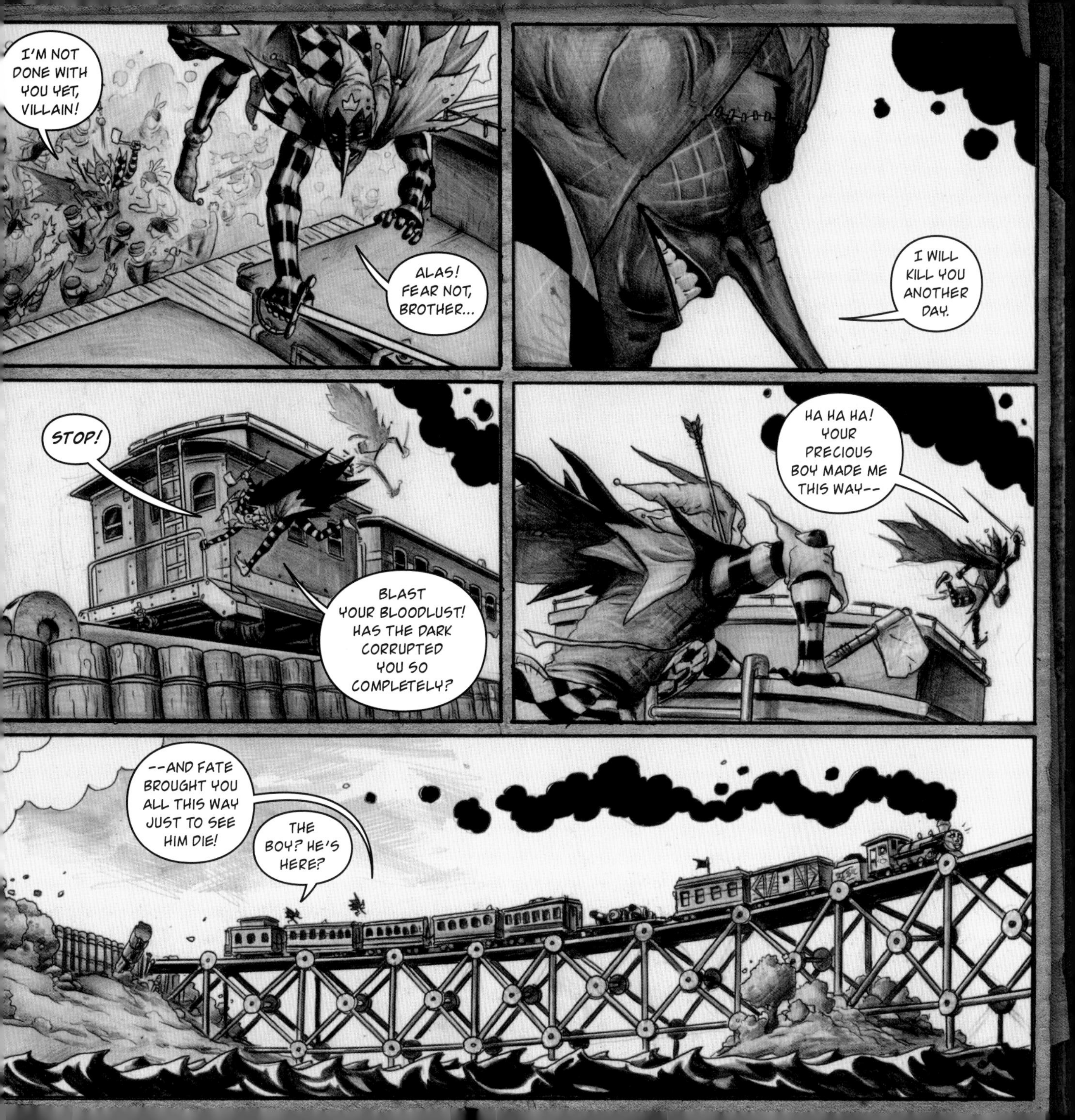
I'M NOT DONE WITH YOU YET, VILLAIN!
ALAS! FEAR NOT, BROTHER...
I WILL KILL YOU ANOTHER DAY.
STOP!
BLAST YOUR BLOODLUST! HAS THE DARK CORRUPTED YOU SO COMPLETELY?
HA HA HA! YOUR PRECIOUS BOY MADE ME THIS WAY--
--AND FATE BROUGHT YOU ALL THIS WAY JUST TO SEE HIM DIE!
THE BOY? HE'S HERE?

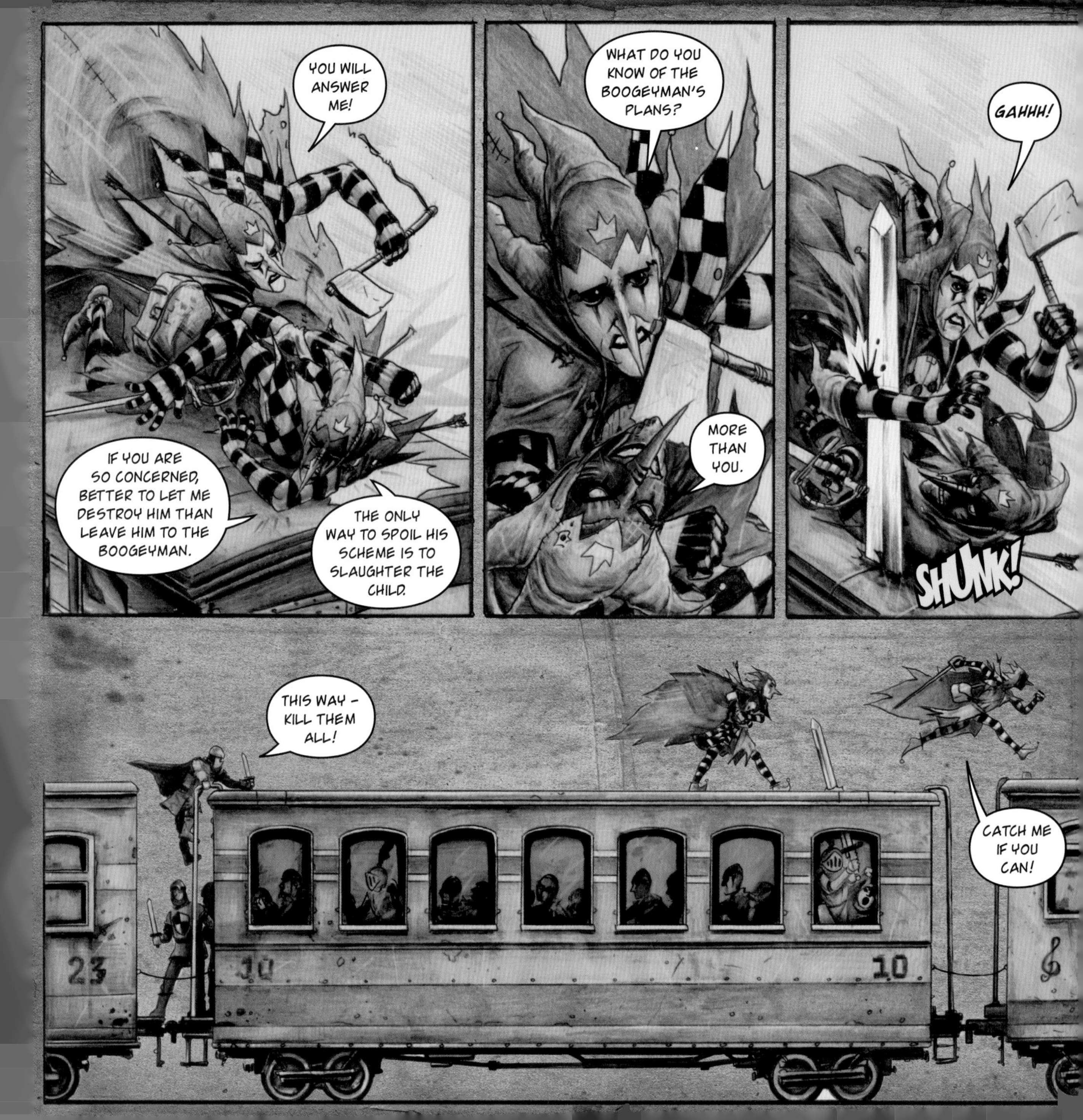
YOU WILL ANSWER ME!
IF YOU ARE SO CONCERNED, BETTER TO LET ME DESTROY HIM THAN LEAVE HIM TO THE BOOGEYMAN.
THE ONLY WAY TO SPOIL HIS SCHEME IS TO SLAUGHTER THE CHILD.
WHAT DO YOU KNOW OF THE BOOGEYMAN'S PLANS?
MORE THAN YOU.
GAHHH!
SHUNK!
THIS WAY - KILL THEM ALL!
CATCH ME IF YOU CAN!
23
10
10

THWIP!

HOW COULD I HAVE BEEN SO BLIND?
..THERE WILL BE NO HAPPINESS UNLESS THE BOY IS RESCUED. HE HAS ALWAYS BEEN THE KEY.

IT FALLS ON ME TO SET THINGS RIGHT.

NO MATTER THE ODDS--

--I WILL NOT FAIL!
KRRRASH!

FOOLS! YOUR FATES ARE ALREADY SEALED!

THERE!

SMASH!
PERFECT TIMING, JESTER.

END OF THE LINE.
MAX... I AM SORRY.
FFT!
BOOOOOOoOOOM!

BOOOoOOM!
WHAT WAS THAT? THE WHOLE CAR JUMPED!

THEY MUST BE FIGHTING ON THE TRAIN. SOUNDS LIKE THEY'RE GETTING CLOSER.
I BET IF I SNEAK OUT THERE, I COULD UNHOOK THE REAR CARS.
THAT'S CRAZY! IF THEY SEE YOU, YOU'RE DEAD!

WELL... I'LL JUST MAKE SURE THEY DON'T SEE ME THEN.
IT'S OUR ONLY CHANCE. LET ME GO. I'M NOT SCARED.

I'LL BE RIGHT BACK.

COME OUT, COME OUT...
...AHA!
THERE YOU ARE.
WHO YOU ARE REMAINS A MYSTERY TO ME, BUT IF THE BOOGEYMAN BROUGHT YOU INTO THE DARK YOU MUST HAVE SOME WORTH.
I WILL TAKE YOUR HEAD TO HIM AS PROOF OF YOUR DEMISE.
DON'T COME ANY CLOSER... I SWEAR... I'LL KILL YOU.
HA HA! WHERE IS YOUR COMPANION? WHERE IS THE BOY I SEEK?
USE YOUR REMAINING MOMENTS WISELY, CHILD.
YOU'LL NEVER GET HIM.

YOU REALLY SHOULD HAVE LISTENED.
NO! YOU--
ME.

I WILL ADMIT TO A CERTAIN LEVEL OF ANNOYANCE WHEN YOU SANK MY NAVY.
GUH!
EVEN THEN, I WAS WILLING TO FORGIVE YOU. IT IS YOUR NATURE TO DESTROY.

HOWEVER...
...ONE THING I WILL NOT TOLERATE IS A THIEF.
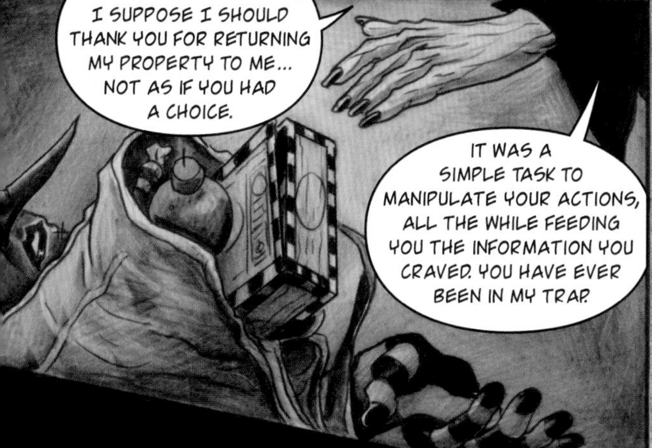
I SUPPOSE I SHOULD THANK YOU FOR RETURNING MY PROPERTY TO ME... NOT AS IF YOU HAD A CHOICE.
IT WAS A SIMPLE TASK TO MANIPULATE YOUR ACTIONS, ALL THE WHILE FEEDING YOU THE INFORMATION YOU CRAVED. YOU HAVE EVER BEEN IN MY TRAP.
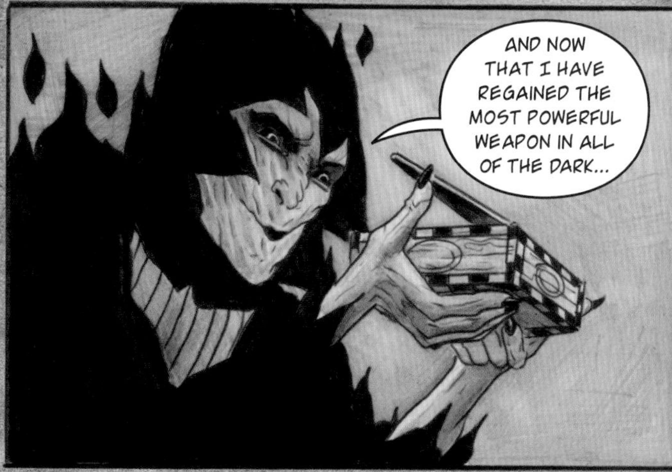
AND NOW THAT I HAVE REGAINED THE MOST POWERFUL WEAPON IN ALL OF THE DARK...
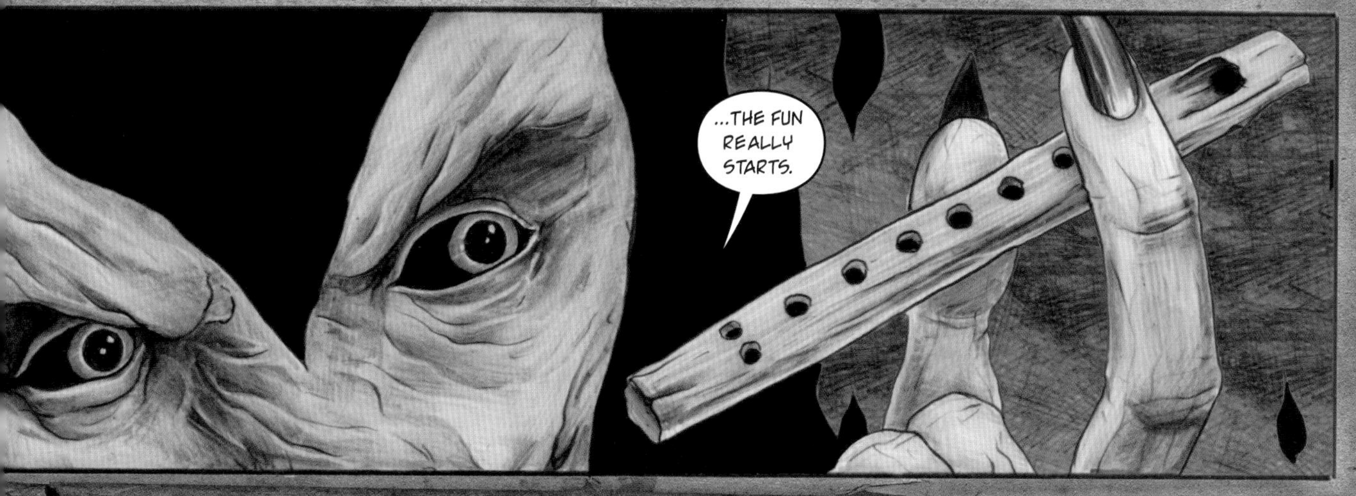
...THE FUN REALLY STARTS.

CREEEEEAK

IT'S OKAY NOW.

WE'RE SAFE. EVERYTHING IS GOING TO BE FINE.
I PROMISE.

Issue #1 Cover Art

C.P. WILSON III

Issue #2 Cover Art

C.P. WILSON III

Issue #3 Cover Art

Issue #4 Cover Art

C.P. WILSON III